The Israelites' journey from bondage to the Promised Land remains one of history's greatest examples of emancipation.

—President Barack Obama

In 1800, President John Adams held the first formal Christmas dinner at the newly built White House. In 1878, President Rutherford B. Hayes observed Easter with a public "Egg Roll" on the White House's South Lawn. It wasn't until 2009 that a US president officially celebrated Passover. This is the story of how it happened.

Malia and Sasha watch White House chefs arrange gefilte fish on fine china. Matzoh ball soup simmers in a sterling silver tureen. Butlers ready carrot soufflé, noodle kugel, and Moroccan charoset.

Bo wags his tail and sniffs as new smells waft through the Old Family Dining Room.

"I bet Bo is wondering why this night is different from all other nights," Sasha says. She has been practicing the Four Questions, which are recited every Passover by the youngest child at the Seder.

Sasha watches as her father's staff members Eric, Arun, and Herbie take their seats at the long table with a Seder plate at the center.

The three young men look around at the splendor and can hardly believe their eyes. Wasn't it only a year ago that they gathered in a windowless room in a hotel basement and ate macaroons out of a can? Now they are celebrating their favorite Jewish holiday with President Barack Obama, his family, and close friends.

How could this have happened?

Next Year
in the
White House

Barack Obama's First
Presidential Seder

by Richard Michelson

illustrated by E.B. Lewis

Crown Books for Young Readers New York

PJ Library Agawam

One year earlier . . .

Eric was homesick.
Arun was hungry.
Herbie was tired.
All three were sad.

It was the first night of Passover, and they were missing their family Seders.

They knew that around the world, Jewish children and parents and grandparents and aunts and uncles and cousins and neighbors and friends were gathering to share a special meal and to retell the story of the Israelites' flight from slavery to freedom.

Eric, Arun, and Herbie could not join their families. They were traveling to a rally in Pennsylvania with Senator Barack Obama, who was running for president of the United States.

It was Eric's job to make sure everyone's luggage was delivered to the right place. What if the senator had to address the nation in his pj's because his sport jacket was missing?

It was Arun's responsibility to film the crowds at the senator's speeches and take pictures of the people who wanted to shake the candidate's hand, give him a hug, or ask him to kiss their babies.

Herbie was in charge of gathering local newspapers for the senator to read so that he could speak about issues that were important to each neighborhood he visited.

Why had Eric, Arun, and Herbie crisscrossed the country for more than a year with Senator Obama? Because they hoped they could help him make America a place where all people—regardless of their race, gender, or religion—would have an equal opportunity to succeed.

But helping others doesn't
mean you don't get
homesick,
or hungry,
or tired.

Eric had an idea. He contacted his cousin who lived nearby and was able to get a box of matzoh, two cans of macaroons, a bottle of Manischewitz wine, and a stack of Haggadahs—booklets of prayers, blessings, and songs celebrating the Israelites' flight to freedom.

Late that night, Eric invited Arun and Herbie to celebrate Passover with him in the only empty room in their hotel. It was small, dark, dingy, and two stories underground.

But they were happy because they were together on this special night and about to retell the story of the Exodus, which is at the heart of every Passover Seder.

Tonight, they would remember the bitter tears the enslaved Israelites shed.

Tonight, they would recount the plagues that fell upon their oppressors and mourn for their enemies who lost their lives.

Tonight, they would cheer their people's daring escape and reaffirm their faith in God's miracles.

Tonight, they would celebrate the sweet taste of freedom and pledge not to rest until all people are free.

Eric remembered how at every Passover, his family opened the front door in the hope that Elijah—the biblical prophet who is invited to every Seder—would return to Earth to spread his message of peace.

Suddenly there was a knock at the door.

Could it be . . . ?

"Hey, is this the Seder? Can I join in?"

Barack Obama missed his wife, Michelle, and their two daughters, Malia and Sasha.

He was homesick,
    and hungry,
        and tired.

He had already promised his girls he would get them a dog to make up for all he had put them through. Some days he was ready to give up his campaign and go home. He knew America had forty-three presidents and not one of them looked like him. No one who was Black had ever come close to being elected president. Even his friends said he was "a candidate with no chance, no money, and a funny name."

"Let all who are hungry come and eat," Eric answered, waving Barack and his closest staff members into the room.

"Friends and strangers are always welcome," Arun added.

"No one should ever be turned away from a Seder," Herbie agreed.

The guests took turns reading aloud from the Haggadah.

Eric read about the nefarious Pharaoh who forced enslaved Israelites to build his stone cities of Pithom and Raamses.

Barack reflected that it was enslaved Black laborers who laid the logs and stones for America's White House.

Arun read about the Red Sea parting so the Jews could cross to freedom. "If it weren't for that miracle," Herbie reminded everyone, "we might still be in bondage."

Barack talked about how the Israelites wandered forty years through the desert to their promised land. "The Exodus story was an inspiration to me and so many of my heroes in the civil rights movement," he explained.

"Imagine forty years of travel without luggage, hotels, or take-out restaurants," Eric joked.

"No cell phones to post pictures of their journey," Arun added.

"And we're complaining after just twelve months on the campaign trail," Herbie admitted.

Barack laughed, then nodded. "The odds were against the Israelites, but patience and hope kept them going when nobody thought they would survive. They believed in hard work and miracles."

It was almost midnight. Everyone was tired, but no one was lonely, hungry, or sad. "We have become a family," Barack said.

"Next year in Jerusalem," Eric called out, raising his glass as the others did the same. It is the hopeful expression for a better tomorrow recited at the end of every Seder.

Barack raised his glass a second time. "Next year in the White House!"

Malia and Sasha listen to their father talk about last year's Seder in a basement. Their mother says it is a miracle that the descendants of two enslaved peoples are now free to share a meal together in the White House, at the invitation of America's first Black president.

The girls are getting restless. Herbie has already hidden the afikomen, the broken piece of matzoh that the girls must find and return for a reward before the Seder can come to an end.

They leave the table, and Bo follows them into the Red Room to begin the search. And what gift do they get in exchange for bringing the afikomen back to the table?

"Look, Bo!" says Malia. Sasha hands him a new chew toy.

Bo barks, and Sasha smiles. "Now Bo definitely knows why this night is different from all other nights."

A Note from Herbie Ziskend, Eric Lesser, and Arun Chaudhary

The purpose of Passover is to tell the story of freedom in your own way and in your time, and so to be included in a book like this is a tremendous honor.

How our impromptu Seder with then-Senator Barack Obama on the 2008 campaign trail came to be—leading to eight more Seders with President Obama and his family in the White House—is an important story to the three of us because it encapsulates so much about what it means to be Jewish.

At its heart, it's about the family you have and the family you make. The Seder you plan meticulously and the one you throw together on the fly. The old traditions we dare not forget and the new ones we create together.

There is no single way to be Jewish; no right way, no wrong way. We are a diaspora people, from many lands and with as many backgrounds. And we come together to tell the story of Passover in many places and situations. Not only in a hotel basement in Harrisburg, Pennsylvania, but in Kyiv and Buenos Aires, in New Zealand and New York, in Johannesburg and Jerusalem.

For eight years, we got to tell that story in the White House, thanks to the generosity of the Obama family. And with the support and participation of so many others over the years, we are thrilled to be able to pass it on to the next generation.

Malia & Sasha:
The Four Questions
מה נשתנה

refill wine

The seder plate is removed from the table and the cups are filled with wine for the second time. The youngest present then asks The Four Questions.

Wherefore is this night distinguished from all other nights?

מַה נִּשְׁתַּנָּה הַלַּיְלָה הַזֶּה מִכָּל-הַלֵּילוֹת?

Any other night we may eat either leavened or unleavened bread, but on this night only unleavened bread;

שֶׁבְּכָל-הַלֵּילוֹת אָנוּ אוֹכְלִין חָמֵץ וּמַצָּה, הַלַּיְלָה הַזֶּה כֻּלּוֹ מַצָּה:

All other nights we may eat any species of herbs, but this night only bitter herbs;

שֶׁבְּכָל-הַלֵּילוֹת אָנוּ אוֹכְלִין שְׁאָר יְרָקוֹת, הַלַּיְלָה הַזֶּה מָרוֹר:

All other nights we do not dip even once, but on this night twice;

שֶׁבְּכָל-הַלֵּילוֹת אֵין אָנוּ מַטְבִּילִין אֲפִילוּ פַּעַם אֶחָת, הַלַּיְלָה הַזֶּה-שְׁתֵּי פְעָמִים:

All other nights we eat and drink either sitting or reclining, but on this night all of us recline.

שֶׁבְּכָל-הַלֵּילוֹת אָנוּ אוֹכְלִין בֵּין יוֹשְׁבִין וּבֵין מְסֻבִּין, הַלַּיְלָה הַזֶּה-כֻּלָּנוּ מְסֻבִּין:

Ma- nish-ta-naw ha-lai-law ha-zeh mee-kawl ha-lay-los? She-b'chawl ha-lay-los aw-nu o-ch'leen chaw-maytz u-ma-tzaw, ha-lai-law ha-zeh ku-lo ma-tzaw. She-b'chawl ha-lay-los aw-nu o-ch'leen sh'awr y'raw-kos, ha-lai-law ha-zeh maw-ror. She-b'chawl ha-lay-los ayn aw-nu mat-bee-leen a-fee-lu pa-am e-chos, ha-lai-law ha-zeh sh'tay f'aw-meem. She-b'chawl ha-lay-los aw-nu o-ch'leen bayn yo-sh'veen u-vayn m'su-been, ha-lai-law ha-zeh ku-law-nu m'su-been.

9 Maxwell House® Haggadah

all move to answer at top of 10

Retelling The Story Of The Exodus
מגיד

Read as a group

lift the matzah

The matzahs are lifted as we recite the following.

This is the bread of affliction which our ancestors ate in the land of Egypt; let all those who are hungry, enter and eat thereof; and all who are in distress, come and celebrate the Passover. At present we celebrate it here, but next year we hope to celebrate it in the land of Israel. This year we are servants here, but next year we hope to be free men in the land of Israel.

הָא לַחְמָא עַנְיָא דִּי אֲכָלוּ אַבְהָתָנָא בְּאַרְעָא דְמִצְרָיִם. כָּל-דִּכְפִין יֵיתֵי וְיֵכֻל. כָּל-דִּצְרִיךְ יֵיתֵי וְיִפְסַח. הָשַׁתָּא הָכָא, לְשָׁנָה הַבָּאָה בְּאַרְעָא דְיִשְׂרָאֵל. הָשַׁתָּא עַבְדֵי לְשָׁנָה הַבָּאָה בְּנֵי חוֹרִין:

Haw lach-maw an-yaw dee-a-chaw-lu a-vaw-haw-saw-naw b'ar-aw d'Mitz-raw-yim. Kawl dich-feen ya-say v'yay-chul. Kawl ditz-reech yay-say v'yif-sach. Ha-sha-taw haw-chaw l'shaw-naw ha-baw-aw b'ar-aw d'Yis-raw-ayl. Ha-sha-taw av-day, l'shay-naw ha-baw-aw b'nay cho-reen.

8

The president and First Lady Michelle Obama continued the tradition of hosting a Seder in each of their next seven years in the White House. Eric, Arun, and Herbie were always invited and conducted the Seder. Here's Eric's Maxwell House Haggadah from the first White House Seder, with his handwritten notes for leading the event.

Who Was at the First White House Seder?

The attendees at the White House Seders during the Obama administration varied from year to year. As Eric Lesser recalls it, the first White House Seder included almost all the people who attended the one on the campaign trail: Barack Obama, Eric Lesser (traveling baggage handler and staff aide), Herbie Ziskend (advance staffer), Arun Chaudhary (traveling videographer), Valerie Jarrett (senior advisor and personal friend of the Obamas), Reggie Love (Obama's aide), Cookie Offerman (advance staffer), Jen Psaki (traveling press secretary), Samantha Tubman (traveling press wrangler), and Eric Whitaker (physician from Chicago and personal friend of the Obamas). Joining them at the first White House Seder were First Lady Michelle Obama and daughters Malia and Sasha Obama, Susan Sher (Michelle Obama's chief of staff and family friend), Neil Cohen and Evan Moore (Sher's husband and son), Melissa Winter (aide to Michelle Obama), Laura Moser (Arun Chaudhary's wife), Martin Lesser (Eric Lesser's father), Lisa Kohnke (member of the White House advance team), and Dana Lewis (aide to Michelle Obama).

The "First Dog," Bo Obama, actually moved into the White House on April 14, 2009, five days after the first White House Seder took place on April 9. While the story in this book is true, and Malia and Sasha did get a doggy chew toy for finding the afikomen, the author has used his official "dog lover's artistic license" and brought Bo to the White House one week earlier than he really arrived. Bo did attend each of the seven other White House Seders.

The White House Passover Seder in 2011. Herbie Ziskend (wearing a white yarmulke) and Eric Lesser (wearing a red yarmulke) are to Barack Obama's right, and Arun Chaudhary is to his left.

More About Black History and Passover

While there is a growing population of Black Jews in America, of the people at the campaign trail Seder in Harrisburg, Pennsylvania, the six who were Black all identified as Christian. Still, the Exodus story has a special place in many Black churches. Harriet Tubman, who helped many enslaved Black people escape to freedom through the Underground Railroad, was called "the Moses of her people." The great Dr. Martin Luther King, Jr., regularly quoted the biblical narrative of the Exodus. In later years, President Obama and his guests would read the Emancipation Proclamation aloud after the meal.

In a speech to the people of Israel on March 21, 2013, President Obama said the following:

I'm proud that I've now brought this tradition into the White House. I did so because I wanted my daughters to experience the Haggadah and the story at the center of Passover . . . a story of centuries of slavery and years of wandering in the desert, a story of perseverance amidst persecution, and faith in God and the Torah. . . .

To African Americans, the story of the Exodus was perhaps the central story, the most powerful image about emerging from the grip of bondage to reach for liberty and human dignity—a tale that was carried from slavery through the civil rights movement into today.

More About Passover

Each year on Passover, Jews all over the world gather with friends and family to read from the Haggadah, a book of songs and prayers celebrating the miracles that allowed the enslaved Israelites to escape from Egypt and taste freedom. Special foods are prepared and set out on a Seder plate. People from different traditions prefer different foods, but they all symbolize the struggles of the past and hopes for the future.

According to the Haggadah, we should try to imagine ourselves as if we were the ones wandering through the desert, frightened and not knowing where we were headed. There are many refugees in that situation today. We repeat the story each year because it is never finished—you too are part of it, and each of us has a responsibility to make the world a better place, where no one is enslaved and everyone has enough to eat.

During the Seder, children are encouraged to ask questions. The youngest child at the table gets to ask the Four Questions, which explore and explain why "this night is different from all other nights."

At the Seder, three matzot (the plural of "matzoh") are placed on top of each other on the table. At a certain point during the meal, the middle piece of matzoh is broken in two pieces. The larger piece, the afikomen (from the Greek word for "dessert"), is hidden in the house, and the children search for it later. The meal is not over until the afikomen is found. In many families, whoever finds it gets a small prize.

A cup of wine is set out for the prophet Elijah. And in many houses, a door is left ajar in hopes that he will visit and bring about an era of peace. At the White House Seder, the cup of Elijah was a kiddush cup (for reciting the blessing over wine) that the First Lady received at the Jewish Museum in Prague.

The Seder traditionally ends with the saying "Next year in Jerusalem." For much of Jewish history, there was no Jewish state, so the Seder closed with the wish for all Jews to be able to return to their homeland, just as they did after leaving Egypt. Since the creation of the state of Israel in 1948, it has become easier for Jews to travel to Jerusalem for Passover. The phrase has come to be a prayer for all people to live in peace in the year to come.

A Recipe for
Flourless Golden Apricot Cake
from Arun Chaudhary

Served at the first White House Seder

12 to 14 servings

INGREDIENTS

CAKE

6 eggs, separated, room temperature

2/3 c. sugar

2 tbsp. fresh orange juice

1-1/2 tbsp. grated orange peel

6 tbsp. matzoh cake meal

2 tbsp. potato starch

1/4 tsp. salt

GLAZE

1/2 c. finely chopped dried apricots

3/4 c. dry white Passover wine

1 c. apricot jam

1 tbsp. honey

2 tsp. grated orange peel

1 tsp. grated lemon peel

1 tsp. fresh lemon juice

3/4 c. sliced almonds, lightly toasted

INSTRUCTIONS

CAKE

1. Preheat oven to 350°F.

2. Using electric mixer, beat yolks and 1/3 cup sugar slowly until the sugar is dissolved and a ribbon forms when beaters are lifted, about 5 minutes.

3. Stir in orange juice and peel.

4. Gradually sift matzoh cake meal and potato starch over mixture, folding them gently into it.

5. Using clean, dry beaters, beat egg whites and salt until soft peaks form.

6. Add remaining 1/3 cup sugar, 1 tablespoon at a time, to egg white mixture and beat until stiff but not dry.

7. Stir 1/4 of this mixture into the yolk mixture until it looks lighter, then fold in the rest of it.

8. Spread batter evenly in ungreased 10-inch springform pan.

9. Bake until top is golden brown and cake springs back when lightly pressed, about 30 minutes.

10. Immediately invert pan on rack. Cool cake completely in pan.

GLAZE

1. Combine apricots and 1/4 cup wine in small heavy saucepan. Let stand until wine is absorbed, stirring occasionally, about 1 hour.

2. Add all remaining ingredients except almonds.

3. Simmer, stirring occasionally, 8 to 10 minutes.

4. Cool until lukewarm.

5. Run a butter knife around side of cake, and remove springform. Cut cake into two layers, using long serrated knife. Slide spatula under cake to release from pan bottom. Transfer bottom layer to large platter.

6. Spread 1/3 of the glaze on it. Top with second layer, and spread 1/3 of the glaze on it. Brush remaining glaze onto sides of cake.

7. Press almonds into glaze around sides and upper edge of cake.

8. Cover cake loosely. Let stand at least 1 hour to absorb glaze.

For Jennifer—this year, next year, and every year.
And for my Martha's Vineyard Polar Bear family—there's no stopping us now.
Special thanks to Eric Lesser and PJ Library for trusting me with this story. —R.M.

Dedicated to all of the peacemakers of humanity —E.B.L.

All rights reserved. Published in the United States by Crown Books for Young Readers, an imprint of
Random House Children's Books, a division of Penguin Random House LLC, 1745 Broadway, New York, NY 10019.

PJ Library

Published in association with PJ Library, a program of the Harold Grinspoon Foundation,
Agawam, Massachusetts.

Crown and the colophon are registered trademarks of Penguin Random House LLC.

Visit us on the Web! rhcbooks.com

Educators and librarians, for a variety of teaching tools, visit us at RHTeachersLibrarians.com

Library of Congress Cataloging-in-Publication Data is available upon request.
ISBN 978-0-593-71158-3 (trade) — ISBN 978-0-593-71159-0 (lib. bdg.) — ISBN 978-0-593-71160-6 (ebook)

The text of this book is set in 20-point ITC Usherwood Std Medium.
The illustrations were created using watercolor on Arches paper.
Book design by Véronique Lefèvre Sweet

MANUFACTURED IN CHINA
10 9 8 7 6 5 4 3 2 1
First Edition

0325/B2917/A8